D1596859

A Catalogue of
the Further Suns

*Précis of Reports Compiled
by the Preliminary Survey Expeditions*

A Catalogue of the Further Suns

Précis of Reports Compiled
by the Preliminary Survey Expeditions

F.J. Bergmann

Gold Line Press

Book design : *Tia Seifert*

www.tiaseifert.com

Published : *Gold Line Press*

http://goldlinepress.com

Gold Line titles are distributed by Small Press Distributions

This title is also available for purchase directly from the publisher

www.spdbooks.org : 800.869.7553

Library of Congress Cataloging-in-Publication Data

A Catalogue of the Further Suns : F.J. Bergmann

Library of Congress Control Number 2017932582

Bergmann, F.J.

ISBN 978-1-938900-24-2

FIRST EDITION

TABLE OF CONTENTS

Overtures	5
Xenoaesthetics	7
Code of Ethics	8
Exobiology I	9
Cultural Exchange	10
Ascendance	11
Point of Departure	12
Unbroken	13
Revisionism	14
Chronomancy	15
Xiphiarchy	16
Cultural Climate	17
Omen	18
Xenotheology I	19
Paleomancy	21
Pavane	22
Cultural Boundaries	23
Hydromorphology	24
Compatibility	25
Oneiroliths	26
Xenolinguistics	27
Fluid	28
Nephology	29
Trek	30
Xenotheology II	31
Exobiology II	32
Absence	33
Exobiology III	34
Duration	35
Acknowledgments	37

... that mixture of contempt and patronizing smugness the Culture found it so difficult not to exhibit when surveying the mistakes of less advanced societies ...

Iain M. Banks, *Consider Phlebas*

OVERTURES

Initially, they seemed to like us,
and were careful not to ask
intrusive questions, but later
they became insistent upon
knowing our emptinesses, and
would enter without warning
just as we had begun to disrobe.
When they caught our chief
zoologist with her favorite
sex toy, they seemed satisfied
and began sharing their private
cultural practices.

Their infants were all given
a wound at birth, and a rough
object (*delrinde*, they called it)
to insert as a plug that kept
the wound open. At seasonal
festivals, they widened their
apertures and thrust in larger
objects. The devout debrided
their wounds each evening
until their clear, viscous blood
puddled on the floor.

We told them that our wound
rituals were private, but when
they noticed scars on some of
us, evidence of surgeries—that
wounds had been *closed*—their
hostility became remarkable.
We had to leave precipitately.
Our departing ship tore a hole
through the skin of clouds.

XENOAESTHETICS

In their language, the word for "poet"
was *troublemaker*; the word for "artist,"
heretic. Any ornamentation—artifice
for its own sake—was blasphemy,
and even adjectives and adverbs were
highly suspicious: they permitted
no embellishments to lard their lean
truths. We had difficulty justifying
our baroque embroideries, not to
mention the floral enamelwork
decorating our pressure suits, until
one of our entomologists had the idea
of explaining Batesian mimicry and
camouflage. Our rollicking ballads
and bawdy limericks caused even more
perturbation. But when we explored
their busy marketplaces, starved eyes
followed us everywhere, and delicate,
whorled ears strained to swivel
toward our songs.

CODE OF ETHICS

During the first millennium, we did nothing
but observe. They were happy to be rid of
stinging insects and some inconvenient
birds. We all hoped that they would come
to their senses. By the time they had lost
the lizard whose intervention was essential
for pollination of the only species of fruit
tree remaining on the smaller subcontinent,
everyone realized we had waited too long.
Other extinctions followed, more swiftly
than our geneticists had believed possible.
We tried to atone by sending teams from
door to door with our personal apologies,
in their last years.

EXOBIOLOGY I

Their hives were castles of yellow sulfur;
their language, a barrage of white noise.
Even their house pets had wheeled feet
or huge faceted eyes the color of moons
rising on our homeworld. Their excreta
glowed in the dark, illuminating convoys
of nocturnal harvest workers and trade
caravans. They still refused to cross
desiccated lowlands where ancient seas
had once swarmed with carnivores
whose monstrous forms were depicted
in the underground temples. In near-
darkness the nervous lamps cast light
upward on thousands of immense replicas
of those extinct creatures, suspended
in eternal twilight. Sometimes the hollow,
lacy shells of golden wire appeared to be
nothing more than ravenous mouths.
We asked, *Why worship what harmed you?*

CULTURAL EXCHANGE

We made initial tight-beam contact from orbit.
They had a highly developed civilization, and
welcomed us eagerly. We landed on a grassy
knoll in a major city, where brass instruments
struck up a jubilant fanfare and children flung
gaudy inflorescences. We removed our helmets
to sunlight and a warm breeze, and the mayor
collapsed before we could even shake his hand.
The cheering died away. Crowds fell in waves
as the plague rippled out from our epicenter.
While we watched helplessly, they deliquesced,
instantly dying on their frilled feet. We recited
dirges in their honor before lifting off. We did
not detect the deteriorating molecular structure
of our ship for months.

ASCENDANCE

They had a specific hierarchy of consumption, and ate nothing
that was not at least six orders of removal from unicellular
status. They had strong views on predation and food
chains as well: parasitism of a higher order by
a lower was anathema. When we pointed out
that they were as dependent on probiotic
microflora as we were, their shame
and subsequent mass suicides
took us completely
by surprise.

POINT OF DEPARTURE

We did not immediately realize
that they could change bodies.
It disconcerted us when a pinafored
child, her tendrils weaving a complex
cat's-cradle, continued the discourse
regarding the cultural implications
of a third gender that we had begun
with an august senior minister
on the previous afternoon, or when
a gawky adolescent would attempt
to entwine one's thigh or genitalia,
enthusiastically critiquing aspects
of one's performance at an earlier
rendezvous with a billowy, butter-
fleshed courtesan. We cautiously
introduced elementary concepts
of democracy and majority rule.
They sent one representative, who
met with our ship's mascot. We
gathered from our pet's parroting
that they had expressed a heartfelt
sympathy for our unfortunate
condition, and wished us better luck
in future endeavors—somewhere else.

UNBROKEN

We thought it was a dead world,
at first. Its albedo was off the scale:
brilliant as a white dwarf, featureless
snow reflected its sun's light back
to the black of space. Glaciers
thousands of meters thick had taken
the place of its seas. But electromagnetic
signals emanated from beneath
the unprinted pages of frozen wastes.
Even after we drilled the shaft
and our envoys descended through
endless strata of cerulean ice
to greet them, they would not admit
the old tales were true: their small
reactors had always kept the frozen
caves habitable, had forever lit
the long tunnels, turquoise darkening
to phthalocyanine in the abandoned
mazes, still nourished the mutant,
stunted crops and the deformed beasts
foraging among frost-feathered ferns
and mosses. *Up* was a direction
in which they no longer believed.
Their universe had become closed:
a labyrinth contained within azure
light as blue as those legendary skies.

REVISIONISM

When they changed their minds,
they changed their forms as well.
Fresh-minted, teneral, a new body—
with new ideas—crept from each
rejected discard. Membranous husks
of former selves wafted sadly
along lonely turnpikes, ghosting
in dying winds, or sagged, deflating,
under NO EGRESS HERE signs.
With each rebirth their exoskeletons
became more heavily armored;
their defense mechanisms more toxic.
Their tongues had a thousand words
for *self-improvement,* but no words
for *guilt,* none for *regret.*

CHRONOMANCY

On the ninth planet, all of them
wanted to become magicians.
They filled their years with retorts
and alembics crusted with dark
oxides, pierced stones and bezoars,
spears of flawed crystal, looking
backward into the terrible past.
They sought to alter time through
their machinations, to repair errors
that had been made long before
their own age, to recover all that
had been lost. They continued
wishing for more wishes, each one
unraveling what another had begun.
Then they were their own undoing.

XIPHIARCHY

Their children were trained to bear
arms from the earliest age at which
they could be induced to ask for them.
All of their toys were dangerous,
leaving wounds on the user as well
as those upon whom they were turned.
They claimed to despise fear, and wore
no armor, but their houses had elaborate
locking systems and they slept with swords
by their sides. They enjoyed hunting
by force of will alone, tracking in snow
(there was always snow) until the moment
when their prey knelt in despair to offer
a shuddering throat to the blade.

*Xiphiarchy: Rule by the sword [Gk xiphos sword + arch(os)
leader]. Thanks to John Koger for the word.*

CULTURAL CLIMATE

At the centers of frozen lakes,
they built crystal palaces of ice
to demonstrate their faith that
climate was immutable. The study
of paleontology and geology was
outlawed; apostates were flung
into glacial rifts and moulins—
but certain academics concealed
ancient records and core samples,
pretended to illicit-but-winked-at
affairs in storage closets to mask
proscribed instruction. Long after
no laws could conceal the cascades
of meltwater or dwindling snows,
it was still fashionable, in those
shrinking, glassy realms, to burn
the wood of forest upon lost forest
in suspended cages of black iron,
to pretend to shudder with cold.

OMEN

It was summer on that joyous world.
They were devouring small birds, roasted
by the dozen, using the violet-feathered skins
to adorn their spines. The Emperor's infantry
wore enameled armor of a visceral green.
The comet hung just above the horizon
before dawn, a pinpoint tailed by a haze
of icy dust. If an alert assistant, tasked with
the Royal Observatory's night shift, had not
spotted it, his rapid promotions to Consultant
Astronomer, His Majesty's Cometologist,
and (for a few days, just before his execution)
Honorary Vizier, would not have occurred;
the weeks-long festival with immense parades
of sentient and animal sacrifices would not
have taken place; the plagues and pathogen
populations would never have swarmed
from the rivers of blood that poured into
shallow marsh deltas. Artist's renderings
were everywhere, taken from descriptions
by those of sufficient nobility to be allowed
brief glimpses through the Imperial Telescope,
since it was not visible to the naked eye.
They could so easily have missed it.

XENOTHEOLOGY I
They worshipped at too many altars.
　　　　　　—Iain M. Banks, *The State of the Art*

When the Imperium decided that
all wars were faith-based, tolerance
was the only answer. It required
everyone to attend weekly services
at churches of every faith within
twenty miles, obeisance credited
with a gold star on their house shield.
Travel time and the duration of some
rites rapidly led to private agreements
of consolidation between previously-
warring denominations. Fidgeting
spawn, linguistic variants,
incredulity, and the interminable
mandatory question-and-answer
sessions following every liturgical
observance were instrumental in
resolving a vast number of once-
irreconcilable schisms,

until certain individuals
figured out a way to profit from
the noble endeavor. Splinter sects
with unscrupulous agendas vied
to place tiny chapels in congested
areas, conducting their sacraments
day and night. The attendant costs
and inconvenience (bribery quickly
entered the picture) led excluded
worshippers to firebomb creeds
perceived as frank charlatanisms.
Violence soon escalated (immense
capital investments were at stake).
The mercenary swordsmen hired
from an outlying world took care not to
destroy any of the religious
edifices responsible for the swollen
augmentation of their revenues.

PALEOMANCY

All they cared for was finding
a beginning. They worked on
unravelings: dissection (messy),
time travel, echolocation of origins
of both sound and light. If noise
interference were eliminated,
it should be possible to hear
the first words of creation—
and watch the Creator's lips,
the expression on that face.
Why, not how.

PAVANE

On that planet, they learned early
the hour and color of their deaths.
There, the Temples of Doom were
the largest industrial complexes,
offering personalized predictions,
with the option of added details
and costly updates, day and night.
Most citizens devoted their lives
to a calm acceptance of their fate,
to composing elegies and epitaphs,
to weaving their own shrouds. But
those who believed that defiance
was possible formed secret cults
devoted to making the demises
of others diverge completely from
times and circumstances foretold.

CULTURAL BOUNDARIES

We came upon a miniature world,
an asteroidlet, really, whose inhabitants
frolicked about our ankles like a wreath
of high-energy particles. Even at a walk,
their slightest motion blurred. Translators
slowed their twittering speech so we could
catch up, late into nights that came too fast,
ended too soon. They held sumptuous feasts
in our honor, but giggled when we nodded off.
It was hard for us to match their enthusiasm.
Shortly, they developed their own transcoders,
and lectured us kindly on our faulty technique.
They overrode our safeties, accessed our files
and equipment specifications, and presented
to us, at the farewell ceremonies, reasoned
critiques of our research protocol and final
theses, as well as redesigned gravitational
thrusters and life-support schemata. They
were too polite to mention the irreversible
biocontamination, or the radiation damage
from the spent fuel we left behind.

HYDROMORPHOLOGY

We found a planet where they had worshiped
water. The faithful were sluiced in clear springs
at birth, showered with rainwater and a gush
of hoarded tears before nuptial flights, lowered
through the ice of a glazed river when they died.
Even the smallest hamlets had built water parks
and ornate fountains. They kept their bubblers
and lawn sprinklers running, never turned off
their faucets, left toilet seats up as a devotional
act. Floods and tidal waves were their miracles.
By the time we arrived, once-undulating hills
had been scoured by streams to gorges visible
from orbital height. The remaining denizens
made pilgrimages into the wastelands, to spit
upon their ancestors' arid graves.

COMPATIBILITY

Their visible spectrum intersected ours,
and their data systems were also binary.
Once within range, our AIs were able
to converse with theirs in nanoseconds
(they expressed temporal duration units
as an infinitesimal part of the total time
elapsed since the universe had come into
being, but no matter). They invited us
aboard their larger vessel—the flagship
of their own survey fleet. We sent a shuttle
with a skeleton diplomatic corps to begin
treaty negotiations. Neither of us had yet
developed antimatter detection capabilities.
Which of us was the true version of being,
and which the mirror?

ONEIROLITHS

There, some could bring back objects
made of physical matter from
the perilous worlds of their dreams:
a madwoman who awoke clutching
a lethal blue flower found only on
mountains thousands of miles away;
a child who, during the week after
her mother's death, was stroked
by an icy astral hand. She put
that pale hand in a valuable box,
kept the box out in plain sight,
always left the house unlocked.
And a man arose late one morning
to find a basalt sarcophagus, sealed
with lead, that could not have fit
through any door, but was somehow
there in his now-crowded bedroom.
He would often put his ear against
the chilly stone and listen to the rustles
and dulcet whispers that came from
inside, suggesting what a good idea
it would be to open it.

XENOLINGUISTICS

When dealing with the most primitive
societies, we began with simple terms: *star,*
stone, stick, hovel, ascarid, and then introduced
locution we thought would empower them:
spiritual guidance, mentorship, trade balance,
legislative model, defense consultants, vermifuge;
but one world had a word that could not be
translated. Our devices initially attempted
to decode it phonetically: *surprise-exclamation/*
generative-organ, and, upon further trials,
buzzed and balked. What could it be?
Struggling through nipple-deep muck,
with an icy rain falling, one of them would
whisper the word, and as it was passed along,
their long, wet ears would brighten to orange
and unfurl for no good reason; or, huddled
around the reeky curl of smoke wisping
from a pathetic fire, they would all begin
chanting it, through pharyngeal orifices
trembling with cold. Even the maimed hunter
dying on a makeshift travois would twitch
in a delirious dance. We isolated individuals
and questioned them exhaustively. Our studies
intensified as they—willfully, we believed—
used the word less and less.

FLUID

There, water was a costly toxin
but hydrocarbons were valueless
due to the ubiquity of teleporters
(high-risk antimatter technology),
so every courtyard had a fountain
that sprayed gouts of fire, colored
on national holidays by chemical
contaminants chosen to correspond
with political loyalties appropriate
to the occasion. On ordinary days,
the flames burned indigo, the hue
of a deep lake under starlight, and
no matter how the ambient heat
made the enraptured air quiver
to tension, they stared at that cool
blue glow as if addicted to poison
or quenching a desperate thirst.

NEPHOLOGY

Their atmosphere was thick, a bisque
of fog. They would not believe we came
from space; they held that nothing existed
beyond the omnipresent, lowering clouds
except heaven. To them, cankerous scars
and burnt oxides on the hull were proof:
our ship had come out of the molten core
of the planet, emerging from a volcano
or one of the bottomless magma abysses
prophesied to glow under the everlasting
polar nights. When we described *stars*,
their puzzled expressions were painful
for us to watch as they creakily unwound
their toroidal coils into open question
marks facing toward a blank gray ceiling,
the end of their world just overhead.

TREK

They spent their lives moving through the gloom
of dim, ever-changing vistas, recording transient
impressions of their itineraries. Those in motile
stages of development carried their sessile spawn
and ancestors in extruded slings. Cultural values
were based on non-visual comparison: *dustier,*
drier, colder, more bitterly scented, much steeper.
Darkness was venerated, in contrast to the days
at the end of each year when the clouds tore apart
and radiation came lancing down on the landscape,
and there was no shield from that bright agony.
They never said that the burdens they bore were
too heavy—nor that they were not heavy enough.

XENOTHEOLOGY II

On that planet, they had learned
to distrust their omens. Miracles
hung in the sky and manifested
from the land and seas around
them daily, but they all kept to
themselves and their appointed
tasks as if they were stone-blind
and deaf, even though our sensors
easily detected their racing pulses,
penetrated their masked temblors.
When our glittering ship floated
low over what had been the glory
of their capital city, our stardrive
harmonics chiming from its fused
ruins, not one of them looked up.

EXOBIOLOGY II

They waited until everyone on the planet
was able to pass a comprehensive test
before turning on the war machines.
The eradication parameters randomly
altered at 28-kilometer intervals, unless
low clouds intervened. Valuable artifacts
had been destroyed, but their most ordinary
objects (worn-out garden tools, old shoes,
blankets, erasers) were carefully arranged
in impregnable bunkers, with data pellets
containing a recording of every being
that had once been alive. They left us
no instructions on how to proceed.

ABSENCE

We searched the whole world
but found no remaining life.
They must have gone extinct
just before our arrival: linens
still dangled on clotheslines;
coffeepots and reactors were
still hot. Besides the household
furniture and appliances, and
the small, collapsing mounds
of ashes, the only trace was
the short array of symbols
on every available surface—
recently painted with blood
and sgraffitoed with shards
of bone. No context was left
for interpretation, and every
document had been burned.
Maybe those unknown motifs
were meant as a challenge, like
a fossil impossibly imprinted
in igneous rock. Perhaps only
a signature.

EXOBIOLOGY III

The problem was that they were, in fact,
entirely different species (to say nothing
of different genera, families—even, some
suspected, planetary origins). Each order
of beings had arisen to similar sentience
via an entirely dissimilar route: the Eaters
had developed intelligence through arduous
requirements imposed by the exigencies
of hunting skills, as their sole prey (dictated
by nutritional needs) became increasingly
difficult to capture; the Eaten, through
evolving the ever-more-sophisticated tactics
necessary to evade their savage predators.
We tried to synthesize sustenance matching
the essential composition of Eaten, in order
to end the cycle of carnage, but our efforts
were superseded by a spontaneous decision
of Eaten to bud a truly discrete subspecies,
carefully selecting from among themselves
members who, by virtue of trivial differences
in physical traits or ideological affiliations,
richly deserved, it was felt, the suffering
inflicted when an Eater slowly digested
a still-living Eaten.

DURATION

We lost the second search party's signal
just beyond the far side of the crater.
Our own signals went unanswered
except for the faint hum reflected
from the clouds. A two-year tour
of duty was at least a year too long.
Just before sunset, the wind rose.
The landscape dissolved in red mist.
We had been guests on that planet
for over three hundred years
without learning each others' languages.
They would come out to listen anyway
when we signaled. They answered
each burst with sharp cries. It seemed
to excite them; perhaps it was like singing.
We wondered if they had a word for *bliss*.

ACKNOWLEDGMENTS

"Absence" first appeared in *Abyss & Apex*

"Ascendance" first appeared in the *Magazine of Speculative Poetry*

"Chronomancy" first appeared in *Abandoned Towers*

"Code of Ethics" first appeared in *Star*Line*

"Compatibility" first appeared in *Star*Line*

"Cultural Boundaries" first appeared in *Asimov's Science Fiction*

"Cultural Climate" first appeared in *Strange Horizons*

"Cultural Exchange" first appeared in *Star*Line*

"Duration" first appeared in *Opium*

"Exobiology I" first appeared in *Apex Magazine*

"Exobiology II" first appeared in *Asimov's Science Fiction*

"Nephology" first appeared in *Ad Astra*

"Oneiroliths" first appeared in *Kaleidotrope*

"Overtures" is forthcoming in *Tales of the Unanticipated*

"Paleomancy" first appeared in *Quantum Realities*

"Pavane" first appeared in *Asimov's Science Fiction*

"Revisionism" first appeared in *Strange Horizons*

"Unbroken" first appeared in *Star*Line*

"Xenoaesthetics" first appeared in *Asimov's Science Fiction*

"Xenotheology I" first appeared in *Atomjack*

"Xenotheology II" first appeared in *Atomjack*

"Xiphiarchy" first appeared in *The Cascadia Subduction Zone*

BIO

F.J. Bergmann edits poetry for *Star*Line*, the journal of the Science Fiction Poetry Association (sfpoetry. com) and *Mobius: The Journal of Social Change* (mobiusmagazine. com), and imagines tragedies on or near exoplanets. Recent work appears in *Analog, Eye to the Telescope, The Future Fire, Pulp Literature*, and a bunch of other places.